FROM EXTROVERT
TO INTROVERT:

I AM EXHAUSTED

From Extrovert to Introvert: I Am Exhausted

Lisa A. Passmore

Copyright © 2024 by Lisa A. Passmore

All rights reserved. No part of this publication may be reproduced, distributed, or transmitted in any form or by any means, including photocopying, recording, or other electronic or mechanical methods, without the prior written permission of the publisher, except in the case of brief quotations embodied in critical reviews and certain other noncommercial uses permitted by copyright law.

ISBN 978-1-62806-447-6 (print | paperback)

Published by Salt Water Media
29 Broad Street, Suite 104
Berlin, MD 21811
www.saltwatermedia.com

Cover image by the author

Dedication

To Logan and Lincoln: I love you 20!

CONTENTS

Breeze 14

Dawn 14

Bloom 14

Pattern 14

Epiphany! 15

Spark 15

Harvest 15

Memory 15

Dusk 16

Return 16

Mirage 16

Ghost 16

Remnant 17

Revive 17

Power 17

Summer 17

Autumn 18

Winter 18

Spring 18

Grandsons 18

Daughters 19

Alaska 19

Prague 19

Chapter in Ireland 19

Relief; CT with the Boys	20
Sedona	20
Reason – Scotland	20
Luck	20
Grammar	21
Rhetoric	21
Music	21
Logic	21
Arithmetic	22
Geometry	22
Astronomy	22
Memory	22
Fading	23
Regret	23
Reflect	23
Erode	23
Regress	24
Depend	24
Blue	24
Violet	24
Yellow	25
Orange	25
Red	25
Green	25
Indigo	26

Ghosts 26

Whales 26

The Ghosts in My Head 27

Haunted House 28

The Deep 28

Silence 29

Ocean 29

We Are Monsters 30

Masks 31

Lighthouses 32

Home 32

Strength 33

There Was a Time 33

Journey 34

Maple Home 36

New Day 36

Monkey 36

Truth 37

Seasons 38

Who am I? 39

Lifespan 40

Forgiveness 41

POEMS

BREEZE

The warm breeze fills me
And replaces the coldness
I feel in my soul

DAWN

When dawn comes, I smile
I have made it through the night
And begin again

BLOOM

I'm waiting to bloom
Into a glorious sight
No one looks away

PATTERN

Patterns reveal
What lies beneath our skin
Fibonacci code

EPIPHANY!

Yikes! Epiphany!
I have discovered so much
A long way to go!

SPARK

Will I feel a spark?
Or will it be inertia?
Electrocution.

HARVEST

A seed well-planted
Will produce a life of grace
And joy as it grows.

MEMORY

Sunday is fun day
Karaoke memory
Singing Bangles songs

DUSK

Dusk is powerful
Becomes night and hard to sleep
Monday is looming

RETURN

Tuesday is third day
Waters and land separate
Return to stasis

MIRAGE

Halfway through the week
Wednesday brings thoughts of travel
Where mirage is real

GHOST

The weekend is nigh
Thursday's nostalgic omen
Is a vengeful ghost

REMNANT

We live for Friday
But every day holds promise
Remnant of the past.

REVIVE

She tried to revive
Her dying interest in life
Saturday appears

POWER

Electricity
Summer storm causes outage
Will cool air return?

SUMMER

My least favorite time
No more summer vacations
Adulting is hard

AUTUMN

I feel best in fall
Now referred to as autumn
Fall is now a verb

WINTER

Snowfall quietens
Then morphs to ice and brown slush
And awakens fear

SPRING

Flowers bloom again
Life captivates my dark heart
And renews my soul

GRANDSONS

The boys are a gift
Energy invigorates
And keeps me going

DAUGHTERS

They each made their choice
One stayed and one had to go
Two halves of my heart

ALASKA

A place bittersweet
I was there first, piece of shit
I'll be there again

PRAGUE

Christmas in Prague, sad
I will never again leave
I'll share holidays

CHAPTER IN IRELAND

New chapters written
More than a new book; I change
I am a new place

RELIEF – CONNECTICUT WITH THE BOYS

My fear took control
I would break the boys somehow
They were safe! Relief.

SEDONA

Sedona crystals
My soul glittered in the sun
Metamorphosis

REASON – SCOTLAND

Do we need reason
To escape our own mind?
Travel to Scotland

LUCK

Is there luck in life?
Is loving worth the gamble?
I am misfortune

GRAMMAR

Semi colon, right?
I am a run-on sentence
My thoughts unending

RHETORIC

A form of discourse
Manipulation or art?
Only writers know

MUSIC

The language of love
Softly swaying in the breeze
Will I ever sing?

LOGIC

Is art logical
How well do we really know
If we are correct?

ARITHMETIC

A girl bad at math
Frees herself from the constraints
Imagination.

GEOMETRY

My shape defines me
Cubist informs my pattern
My body; Buddha

ASTRONOMY

I live to look up
Absorb the constellations
and become a star

MEMORY

Memory fading
Forgiving the transgressions
Become whole again

FADING

The fading sunset
Moves into the blackest night
I am not afraid

REGRET

Does one feel regret
When one chooses to be free
From those who would hurt?

REFLECT

Reflecting my pain
You have mirrored my sadness
And changed it to joy

ERODE

The beaches erode
My home closer to the sea
And will disappear

REGRESS

Onward and upward
There is no time to regress
Only growth and peace

DEPEND

Codependency
Was the label but untrue
Manipulation

BLUE

My childhood blue
My adolescence light blue
My life now bright blue

VIOLET

Wonka Violet
The mean girls in my life, banned
Decimated their color

YELLOW

The color of sun
The blinding rays soothe my eyes
Behind sealed lids

ORANGE

Knock, Knock. Who is there?
Orange, the color of life
I taste the sweetness

RED

Eyes blaze with fire
Turmoil caused by monsters
Engulfed by hot rage

GREEN

The color of greed
Money's the root of evil
And makes the world cry

INDIGO

I am a purple
Born into blue's monster clan
Never to be changed

GHOSTS

I see the shadows
The quick movements barely seen
But I understand

WHALES

Fish
with Air
in rings as
an aquatic net
mimicking Fibonacci code

THE GHOSTS IN MY HEAD

If only walls could speak
They would tell tales of unspeakable horrors
The stains on the walls left in effigy
Burdened by the faded floral accents
Whispers carelessly floating like dust mites in dim sunlight
Words felt like sharp knives cutting in the middle of the night
Tearing through the viscera filling me with pent
Up rage hot like fire increasing the clarity
Of the truth meant to prepare me for slaughter
Afraid of the stares making me look like a freak
The autumn air's temperature turning bleak
Awaiting the end of October when the neighborhood's terror
Is underneath the costumes portrayed with a levity
Belied only by the sound of laughter meant
To be a cherished tradition where candy and giggles hide fright
Stories and images knocking about my head and might
Be meaningful to me but look to another insouciant
And create misunderstood scripts with no analogy
And describing this language to the unenlightened makes me suffer
Unintended consequences where I end up in a fetal position and weak
All I really want to do is rise up and shriek
Waiting for the pain and gore from the razors
Tongues wagging of those who religiously practice enmity
Becoming something less than sentient
In the end becoming an acolyte

HAUNTED HOUSE

Home is never a word I used
Always moving from apartment to house
Until I found the place I will never leave
Never needing a solid geographical location
This place is isolated where transforming
Energy is safely guarded by
Demons who understand the need to grow and
Heal by delving into the dark shadows
Of my soul where I
Used to hide. No longer do I feel the need to run from the
Safe place I now call home where my
Emotions live mingling with the ghosts of my past

THE DEEP

The deep blue sea breathes
And absorbs parts of my soul
Into the blackness

SILENCE

The silence was like something that grew deeper and deeper by the moment
The chasm growing wider and wider with every unspoken word
How did we get here?
There must've been love at some point, right?
We have a child
We have a life
Why am I not enough?
I call your bluff
Your quiet cuts like a knife
Through the sorrow, I have to smile
And lie awake through the dark night
of the soul when your anger is severe
and cannot be soothed by balmy herbs.
Continue the stillness of torment

OCEAN

Why do you call me?
I live so close yet so far
Will you carry me away?

My call beckons you
I can soothe your troubled soul
With silence and love

WE ARE MONSTERS

Necessary Evil
Necessary Mores
Mores Collide
Mores Divide
Divide the people
Divide the land
Land of my fathers
Land where they died
Died for their sins
Died for their country
Country of lies
Lies borne of fear
Fear controls
Fear extolls pain
Pain requires numbing
Pain brings peace
Peace begets contentment
Peace is love
Love is a drug
Love feels like a thousand hugs
Hugs heal
Hugs make us feel
Feel what scares us
Feel to become numb
Numb is the new norm
Numb chases away the storm
Storm has the power
Storm passes
Passes are given to the elite

Passes are currency
Currency controls
Currency patrols
Patrols dominate the masses
Patrols kick their asses
Asses rise to the top
Asses misuse perceived power
Power usurped from us
Power put under a glass
Glass ceilings are broken
Glass wings are stolen
Stolen identities and cultures
Stolen land and heritage
Heritage is expanding
Heritage notwithstanding
Notwithstanding they remain calm
Notwithstanding they remain clever
Clever minds
Clever hearts
Hearts...
Minds...

MASKS

Narcissist nightmare
What happens when the ruse fails?
And the demon grows

LIGHTHOUSES

Lighthouses provide safety and illumination during a storm
I find myself wanting to be there wrapped up in a warm
grey tower where ascending the steps feels akin to
Heaven, needing to find a way
through to the other side where
human fears push me ever closer to the
ocean where sharks play and turtles glide
underwater
Salty teardrops fall from my
eyes when I see the morning
sun through my camera lens

HOME

There was a place my heart longed to see
A place not located on a map
A place found only in my mind
A place I was safe
A place I was loved
A place I called home

STRENGTH

Sheer
Terror
Relishes
Enveloping
Narcissists
Going
Through
Hell

THERE WAS A TIME...

There was a time I lived the perfect summer
We traveled together
The boys
The photographs
The laughter
The bus
The bond
And when we returned
The mall
The sun
The Frisbee
The music
The friendship
We two
Magic

JOURNEY

The journey of life is hard
The journey of love is sacred
Sacred love spells cast
Sacred love poems written
Written in flowery frenetic script
Written before we enter our crypts
Crypts encase our souls
Crypts encase our bodies
Bodies remain and spirits rise
Bodies decay and become inspiration
Inspiration morphs into art
Inspiration is our essence
Essence determines character
Essence removes the barriers
Barriers block the joy
Barriers replaced by toys
Toys return childhood
Toys belong in book nooks
Nooks hide us from the monsters
Nooks repel martyrs
Martyrs wear masks
Martyrs bask
Bask in the glory of grandiose machinations
Bask in their own ambiance
Ambiance meant to control
Ambience as loud as a pistol
Pistol aimed
Pistol fired
Fired up about nonsense

Fired up for show
Show dogs
Show her your world
World caving in
World drenched in sin
Sin saves
Sin waves
Waves crash on the beach
Waves make change
Change can be achieved
Change is currency
Currency in a stock market
Currency in a meat market
Market love for sale
Market is monopolistic competition
Competition for love
Competition for money
Money for travel
Money unravels
Unravels...
Travel...

MAPLE HOME

Summer
I felt safe there
Your parents showed me love
I will never forget that time
I changed

NEW DAY

wake up at dawn
See the sun rise and smile
take that sun with me every day
New life

MONKEY

Musings
Only
Need
Kind
Energy and
Yearning

TRUTH

I sometimes feel the growing distance
Thirty-three years with my heart and soul
I get to see the ethereal shine of her brilliance
And because of her I now feel whole
When this life ends, I will begin the new role
preparing me for my demise
Where I will inevitably have to give up control
and no longer compromise
When I am with you I will no longer suffer in silence
I will begin to shout the virtues I extoll
For I have already paid the penance
for the parts of me the monsters stole
no longer hiding in the hole
hidden from prying eyes
attempting to cajole
only to realize
I have been the one who made the difference
and no longer needing to patrol
paths where you wait with the patience
of an angel for me to stroll
past you with eyes black as coal
and the warmth of the sun to strategize
exactly what it will take out of me to roll
with the flow, so to speak and attempt to summarize
the past sins, find a process allowing me parole
from the jail, I had no business being confined to and chastise
me in hopes you can use to burn me in effigy, tethered to a pole
surrounded by songs meant to condescend and patronize

SEASONS

I wish I had the same love of summer others do
I wish I had the same love of summer others do
My heart and soul belong to autumn
My heart and soul belong to autumn
Summer belongs to others' hearts who wish I had
The same soul love of autumn I do

The smell of cooking food does not compare to burning leaves
The smell of cooking food does not compare to burning leaves
Crisp autumn air restores my soul Summer breeze stifles
Crisp autumn air restores my soul Summer breeze stifles
The burning food smell restores my soul as the crisp
autumn leaves do not compare to the summer breeze

A swim in the pool is akin to a bath; A hike in the forest is restorative
A swim in the pool is akin to a bath; A hike in the forest is restorative
The sand is everywhere. Crunchy tattered leaves cling to me
The sand is everywhere. Crunchy tattered leaves cling to me
A restorative swim in the pool where sand is everywhere is akin to the
bath of crunchy tattered leaves clinging to me

Summer thunderstorms are angry and judgmental. Indian summer is bliss
Summer thunderstorms āre angry and judgmental. Indian summer is bliss
Perhaps the difference between the season is a reflection of me

Perhaps the difference between the season is a reflection of me
Perhaps a seasonal reflection is the difference
between a blissful Indian summer reflection and an angry
summer thunderstorm

WHO AM I?

I'm not feeling like myself today.
Can you remind me who I am?
I'm not feeling like my best self today
Can you remind me who I'm trying to be?
I'm not feeling like someone I want to be
Can you show me what she looks like?
I'm not feeling joy today
Can you let me know what that feels like?
I'm not looking in the mirror anymore
Can you tell me what I look like?
I'm not feeling love today
Can you speak like you love me?
I'm feeling very insecure today
Can you change my mind?
I'm feeling in every fiber imposter syndrome symptoms
Can you validate my intelligence?
Can you?
Will you?

LIFESPAN

spring blossoms smell pure and the sunlight warms
a prelude to the suffocating sultriness of summer
she begins to develop her personality and charms
her toothless smile belies the tricycle trauma which becomes her
essence, revealing her entire soul with her bright hazel eyes
shining until the light is extinguished replaced by cries
a prelude to the suffocating sultriness of summer
autumn days are ahead and she's not sure she will survive
she takes this time to remain inside finding distractions to
recover
from the heat permeating the heavy air where she became a
sacrifice
to those who would traumatize and manipulate
her until she identified those she would annihilate
autumn days are ahead and she's not sure she will survive
cooler days prevail and she learns protection and love
and prepares herself for the time of her demise
with laughter and joy and gratitude for those above
who guide her every day
allowing her to move safely from concrete to gray
cooler days prevail and she learns protection and love
the sheets of ice blanket her in serenity
soft as the wings of a dove
preserving her exponentially growing divinity
knowing this life is nearly complete
when she will no longer feel weak
the sheets of ice blanket her in serenity
her former body no longer in pain
ready to celebrate with her angels for eternity

where some days bring the soft rain
of spring
crashing
her body no longer in pain
moments of a sweet summer memory
come slamming through again
no longer causing injury
now smelling like leaves burning
tasting like apple cider with all the seasons merging

FORGIVENESS

Feelings
Overwhelm
Reality
Gauging
Intuitive
Vibes
Even when
Not
Entering
Sacred
Silence

ABOUT THE AUTHOR

Dr. Lisa Passmore is a Florida resident who is healing and becoming a better citizen of the Universe. She has spent the last 20 years as a nurse cultivating her creativity in various ways including photography, writing, and painting. Lisa's love for her two grandsons, daughter, and son-in-law inspire her every day.

www.ingramcontent.com/pod-product-compliance
Lightning Source LLC
Chambersburg PA
CBHW070803050426
42452CB00012B/2473